How to Stop Employee Resistance to Change

By Robert Tanner, MBA

Copyright © 2018 | Business Consulting Solutions LLC

All rights reserved, worldwide. No part of this book may be reproduced, stored in a retrieval system, or transmitted in any form or by any means, electronic, mechanical, photocopying, recording, scanning, or otherwise, without the prior written permission of the publisher.

Contents

OVERVIEW 1

1 RESISTANCE TO CHANGE: WHAT MANAGERS MUST KNOW 3
    The Fairy Tale about Change That's Destroying Managers' Careers 3
    Insider Secrets about Employee Resistance to Change 5
    Change Scenario: A Change Effort Gone Badly 6
    Root Cause Analysis: Pinpointing the Causes of Employee Resistance to Change© 11

2 RESISTANCE TO CHANGE: HOW MANAGERS CAN RESPOND 13
    Why You Can't Ignore Employee Resistance 13
    What You Can Do About Employee Resistance 16
    Change Scenario: What Should Have Been Done 17
    Benefit Analysis: Explaining the Value of Your Change Effort© 20

3 RESISTANCE TO CHANGE: HOW MANAGERS CAN SUCCEED 22
    Neutralizing Resistance to Change 22
    Transforming Employee Resistance into Employee Support 25
    Change Scenario: Getting it Right 26
    Change Implementation Analysis: Building a Powerful Change Rewards Program© 30

CONCLUSION 31
ACCESS TO END OF CHAPTER TOOLS 33
ADDITIONAL RESOURCES 34
    Cheat Sheet: 4 Insider Secrets to Counteract Resistance to Change© .. 35
    Cheat Sheet: 5 Best Practices for Effectively Communicating Your Change Effort© 36
    Chart: Why People Resist Change© 37
LINKS TO LEADERSHIP RESOURCES 38
ABOUT THE AUTHOR 39
DISCLAIMER 40
USE OF THIS MATERIAL 41
REFERENCES 42

OVERVIEW

If you are experiencing employee resistance to change, then I have good and bad news for you! The **good news** is that even the most experienced managers face employee resistance to change.

The **bad news** is that employee resistance to change is something you should expect. It comes with the territory!

In fact, depending upon the scope of your change, stopping employee resistance to change can be like whack-a-mole (as soon as you stop one instance of employee resistance, another instance of employee resistance occurs) (Whack-a-Mole, 2018).

Employee resistance to change is common today. It occurs because the business environment is drastically different from earlier times.

Change today is complex and rapid!

Change is also difficult because often it is chaotic or it is disruptive.

Chaotic change is anything that breaks the environment in which you are operating in an immediate and perceptive way. Often, chaotic change is unpredictable and rapid. Disruptive change is anything that structurally changes the way you run your business. Often, disruptive change can be predictable and manageable with foresight (Berkman, Olivia, 2018).

Despite the difficulties of implementing change today, the harsh truth is that others in your organization still expect you to be successful at making it occur. Your boss, peers, and employees do not really care if the change is chaotic or disruptive. They just want you to get it done!

For you, change and leadership are interconnected. You cannot lead your employees if you cannot get them to accept the need for change. Further, you cannot get your employees to change if they are committed to resisting your efforts to lead them.

To be successful, you will have to develop strategies to stop employee resistance to change.

If you are unable to understand the cause of a problem it is impossible to solve it. (Naoto Kan)

1 RESISTANCE TO CHANGE: WHAT MANAGERS MUST KNOW

The Fairy Tale about Change That's Destroying Managers' Careers

Research shows that up to 66% of organizational change efforts fail. A significant obstacle that contributes to this failure is the widespread belief that many managers have about change and their employees. Specifically, many managers have adopted the myth that people naturally resist change.

Here is the truth: people do not naturally resist change. This widely held view of change leadership is a fairy tale!

Sadly, managers are not the only group of business

professionals that hold to this false view of change. In fact, many consultants and leadership experts also hold and promote this false view about employee resistance to change (Tanner, Robert, 2017).

The problem with this false view about employee resistance to change is that it is destructive — both to the change effort itself and ultimately to the careers of the managers who believe this myth.

Consider the following: When managers accept this fairy tale, they interact with their employees as if their employees are opponents who they must restrain.

Whether these managers force their employees to submit by overpowering them or by manipulating them, the result is the same. It creates a destructive cycle as it causes employees to resist the change even more.

Here is what happens: Employees realize their managers are forcing them to submit to the changes. These employees respond by being defensive and apprehensive about the change effort.

Over time, this type of continuing interaction causes the managers and the employees to take part in a continuing tug-of-war.

The result for these managers is a change outcome that at worse fails completely or at best is below average. When this occurs, managers' find that they have damaged their organizational reputations — as others view them as ineffective leaders of their employees.

If you need to implement a change effort, there is an alternative for you. You do not have to go down this destructive leadership path.

The first thing to do is to understand the truth about employee resistance to change.

Here are two facts:
1. Employees **do not** resist change that they believe is in their best interest.
2. However, employees **will** resist change when they believe that the results will not be positive for them.

Here is a story that I share in my leadership training that proves my point that people do not naturally resist change:

After the end of a tough week in the office, you arrive home and eat a quick meal and collapse on your bed. Early the next morning, you check your mailbox and find that you have a registered letter at the postal office. You get annoyed and reluctantly get dressed to go pick up this "special letter" on what is supposed to be your day off.

On the way there, you say to yourself that this better not be another trick sales offer from that vendor trying to sell you something for your house. You arrive at the postal office and you stand in line for what seems like forever. You finally get to the representative who has your mail and you grumble that you are there to pick up a registered letter.

He gets your letter, gives it to you, and when you look at it you can't believe what you have received. You say to yourself that this can't be what you think it is. You start visibly shaking as you quickly open the letter.

As you read the letter, your whole attitude changes. You go from being grumpy to being excited. By the time you get to the end of the letter you are jumping up and down and yelling with delight. You just won a national sweepstakes contest and the award is one million dollars.

Now I have just one question for you: Are you going to resist this change (Tanner, Robert, 2018)?

Insider Secrets about Employee Resistance to Change

Since employees do not resist change that is in their best interest, why would they resist their manager's efforts to implement changes that appear to be clearly beneficial to the organization?

This question leads to the second myth about employee resistance to change. This is the mistaken belief that employee resistance to change is often irrational.

Employee resistance to change is rarely irrational. In fact, employee resistance to change comes from a perspective that makes perfect sense to those employees who are resisting their manager.

Employee resistance to change often comes from a divide

between employees and their manager. This divide can come from differing perspectives, interests, or intent about the expected outcomes of a proposed change.

In summary, if employees are resisting your efforts to make a change, then they have some reason for believing that the change you want to make is not in their best interests.

Isolating the different reasons why employees are resisting your efforts might seem like an impossible task. Fortunately, organizational development work shows that there are eight common reasons why employees resist change.

They are as follows:
1. Loss of status or job security in the organization
2. Poorly aligned (non-reinforcing) reward systems
3. Surprise and fear of the unknown
4. Peer pressure
5. Climate of mistrust
6. Organizational politics
7. Fear of failure
8. Faulty Implementation Approach (Lack of tact or poor timing) (Tanner, Robert, 2018)

To stop employee resistance to change, you will need to identify the real reason(s) why your employees are resisting your change effort. The reasons may be different from what your employees communicate to you directly. Their reasons may also be different from your initial thoughts.

Keep in mind that employee resistance to change may not have a common group consensus. Employees often have different reasons for resisting change. For this reason, you will also have to do an individual analysis of each of the affected employees.

Let's explore this further with a real-world workplace example.

Change Scenario: A Change Effort Gone Badly

Assume that John, a department manager, wants to implement new software to respond to the CEO's strategic directive for the entire organization of reducing costs and simplifying processes.

The change that John wants to make is extensive. It will require an extensive overhaul of existing departmental processes. It will require replacing the current software that has been in use for ten years with new software from an external vendor.

The benefits of the change that John wants to make are also extensive. If John's change effort is successful, it will reduce the department's labor costs significantly with a reduction in overtime costs. It will also be simpler to use.

As John prepares to present his idea to his team of 10 employees at their weekly team meeting, he can barely contain his excitement.

When John does meet with his employees, his presentation covers the following:
- The software will allow the department to meet the CEO's cost cutting and work simplification directive.
- The software will allow the department to do more.
- The software will eliminate several current complex processes
- The software will reduce the amount of overtime required to do the department's work for the organization.

Throughout his presentation, John visually scans the room and the responses of his employees shock him:
- His resident expert employee for the current system is visibly upset. The expert employee frowns and squirms in his chair throughout John's presentation. When John asks him to speak up, the expert employee says that he believes that the software is too costly and that it is really not that much of an improvement over the current system.
- Two essential employees who perform all of the department's information technology work look at the expert employee, the other employees, and at each other with nervous quick glances. When John asks for their input, they provide a neutral response that is unenthusiastic. They say that they are not

sure if the software will work as the vendor promises. They explain further that they are willing to review the product to see if it can deliver what it promises.
- Finally, John's remaining seven employees look at him with little emotion. When he asks for their input, they decide not to give him their opinions. Instead, they respond by saying that they do not have enough information to give him an informed response.

As he really needs their support to make the change happen, John does what he can to hide his irritation from his employees. He postpones any action on his proposal for a future meeting.

Analysis

As John goes home, he thinks about what occurred earlier in the day. Replaying the meeting in his mind, John realizes he should resist the temptation to label his team as being a bunch of resistant employees. As he thinks about his presentation, he can see that he did present the overall benefits of the software to the group.

However, John also realizes by their reactions to his presentation that he did not do any advance work to identify potential employee resistance to change. This left him in a vulnerable position with his employees, as he was unprepared to address their resistance to his change effort.

Instead of thinking of them as employees who have been in their jobs too long and that need to be replaced, John decides to look further for the reasons for their resistance.

As John gathers information over the next few days, here is what he finds:
- John's expert employee is resisting John because he realizes that the new software will reduce his status among his peers as the resident expert. The expert employee also worries whether he will be able to keep his job once John implements the new software (***reason for resistance***: loss of status or

job security in the organization).
- John's two essential information technology (IT) employees actually are open to using the new software since the vendor has a good reputation. They recognize however that the rest of the employees have reservations about John's proposal. Since they need the good will of their fellow employees to do their jobs, the IT employees do not want to support John's proposal openly until the rest of the group supports it (**reason for resistance**: peer pressure).
- John's remaining employees who showed no enthusiasm for his proposal are still upset about the last change effort the CEO made the organization complete. It was chaotic and it required them to work extensive overtime to meet that directive. Even though they know the CEO's directive is behind John's push for the new software, they are resistant to a change of this size. They believe this change effort will be worse than their prior experience given its scope. They want John to do something else (**reason for resistance**: climate of mistrust).

By managing his emotions (Tanner, Robert, 2018) and doing some strategic information gathering and analysis, John has identified valuable information. He now knows why his employees acted as they did during his presentation.

While John does not personally agree with how they view this situation, he at least now understands their thinking. He recognizes that their resistance to change makes perfect sense to them given their perspectives.

Solution

So, let's bring this back to you and your change effort.

What can you do to avoid the mistakes that John made?

The first step to stop employee resistance to change is to identify the real reasons (root cause analysis) why your employees might resist your change effort. This is a proactive step. It is something that you will do before you launch your change effort.

To do a root cause analysis you need to gather data about your change effort, your organization, and your employees. This involves communication, observation, and analysis.

A root cause analysis often involves the following:
- Doing two-way communication with your employees (open-ended questions, listening, paraphrasing)
- Observing work place operations (interactions among employees, work transactions, etc.)
- Reviewing relevant departmental data and metrics (reports, operational data, written information)

Use the tool at the end of this chapter to conduct your own root cause analysis.

Key Points

If you do not understand the real reasons why your employees are resisting your efforts to make change, then you will not be able to stop their resistance. There are eight common reasons why people resist change. Individual employees can have different reasons for opposing a change effort.

Here are some key points to understand about employee resistance to change:
- Employees do not naturally resist change. They will accept change that they believe is in their best interests.
- Employees will resist change however if they believe that it will make their organizational situation worse.
- Employee resistance to change is rarely irrational. From your employees' perspectives, their resistance makes perfect sense to them.

Root Cause Analysis: Pinpointing the Causes of Employee Resistance to Change©

Overview

Employee resistance to change comes from their belief that the change that they now have to implement is not in their best interests. To handle team member concerns, it is important that you anticipate, understand, and respond to their concerns appropriately. If you do not, you may not get the results that you need.

Instructions

Using the worksheet on the next page, identify the primary reason why employees may resist your change effort. Use a separate sheet for each of your employees and brainstorm the reasons why each of your individual employees might potentially resist your change effort.

Here again are the eight common reasons why employees resist change:
1. Loss of status or job security in the organization
2. Poorly aligned (non-reinforcing) reward systems
3. Surprise and fear of the unknown
4. Peer pressure
5. Climate of mistrust
6. Organizational politics
7. Fear of failure
8. Faulty Implementation Approach (Lack of tact or poor timing)

Worksheet: Pinpointing the Causes of Employee Resistance to Change©

Employee Name:_____

1. What exactly has this team member said or done that makes you feel they may resist your change effort? *(Describe their actions in specific terms. What are the reasons why you view them as a potential resistor to your change effort?)*

2. Which of the eight common reasons why people resist change will be the primary reason for this employee to resist your change effort?

3. What evidence do you have to support your position (in Question 2) about the primary reason why this employee may resist your change effort? *(Describe what you have seen, heard, etc. that supports your position that they may resist you.)*

4. What can you do to stop this employee from resisting your change effort? *(What proactive steps can you take to get them to support your change effort?)*

You never get a second chance to make a first impression (Will Rogers)

2 RESISTANCE TO CHANGE: HOW MANAGERS CAN RESPOND

Why You Can't Ignore Employee Resistance

From the Change Scenario in Chapter 1, it is clear that John had a good idea for his department about how to comply with the CEO's strategic directive. What John did not have was a proper understanding of his employees' concerns about implementing the new software, however. This made for a bad start for his implementation of his change effort.

Since first impressions matter, John should have done some preliminary work before talking to his employees about the change that he wanted to make. Specifically, he should have done a root cause analysis before his presentation to his employees.

John's main failing was the following:

He explained the benefit of the change to the group as a whole but he never even considered how the change would affect his employees individually.

The harsh truth is that it is hard for employees to be excited about any change if all that they see for themselves are negative consequences (Tanner, Robert, 2018).

By not doing this pre-work, John made his future change implementation efforts more difficult. Since the introduction of his change effort produced a negative response from his employees, their resistance will only intensify with time. John has some cleanup work to do to fix this situation.

John's situation is not unique. Many managers approach change as John did.

These managers operate from a false understanding that all that they need to do is explain the following for change to occur:

- Change has to happen because senior leadership says so
- Change has to happen because it will help the organization

As the Change Scenario shows however, implementing change is far more complex.

In fact, managers in organizations tend to underestimate the negative impact of employee resistance on the success of a change effort. This is especially true when the senior leadership of an organization has taken a strong position on the necessity of change (as John's CEO did in the Change Scenario).

Many senior leaders (like John's CEO) understand that their active involvement is necessary to implement significant change across an organization. Senior leaders are often most active in the beginning stages of a change effort. Their involvement usually begins with sponsorship (communicating the need for change).

An effective communication message from senior leadership creates a sense of urgency (Tanner, Robert, 2018). (Urgency alerts the organization that change must occur quickly).

Senior level involvement in creating urgency is essential to the success of a change effort.

The success of this step can lead a lower level manager (like John) into a false sense of security about the future success of his or her departmental change effort, however. This happens when a lower level manager (like John) believes that these senior level directives are sufficient to force his or her employees to cooperate with a change effort.

In reality, employees readily accept change only when they believe that the change is in their best interests. Employees will find ways to resist a change that they believe is not in their best interests — regardless of what the big boss says.

This fact of organizational life is difficult for some managers to accept. These managers reason that since the employees' jobs are in jeopardy the employees will reluctantly comply and make the needed changes.

This perspective of organizational change assumes that employees have little power in these situations. Employees are not powerless pawns in an organization.

Here are five ways that employees can (and do) resist obeying management's directive to change:

1. They leave (they voluntarily leave the organization)
2. They dig in and fight (they resist openly or indirectly)
3. They withdraw their support (they only do what is required)
4. They withhold information (they refuse to share critical information with managers that will lead to better change outcomes)
5. They damage reputations (they share their discontent with others) (Tanner, Robert, 2017)

So, what does this mean for you?

As you work to implement a change effort, it helps to highlight in your communication with your employees that senior leadership is requiring the organization to make changes to support specific directives. You can then build on this point by showing how your specific change effort aligns with senior leadership's directives.

Your communication that senior leadership wants change has limited implementation value however! It is useful for getting the attention of your group but it is less helpful for keeping them actively engaged and supportive over the long term.

To achieve continuing employee engagement and cooperation with your change effort, you will have to expand your communication message to address other critical information areas.

We will review these areas in the next section.

What You Can Do About Employee Resistance

When you are dealing with employee resistance to change, it can seem overwhelming. Sometimes you feel that you are making progress in gaining their cooperation only to later feel that you have made no progress at all.

Keep in mind however that employees do not resist change that is in their best interests. (While keeping their jobs is in their best interests, you will need more than threats to stop their resistance to change. In fact, continual threats intensify employee resistance. No one likes to be threatened!)

Your goal is to gain the willing cooperation of your employees to work with you to implement change. If you do this, it will make your work life far easier and it will help you to implement your change effort successfully.

So, how do you get there?

How do you get your employees to stop resisting change?

The key is to address what is most important to your employees for the change effort that you want to implement. Specifically, while your employees care about what is good for the organization, their first concern individually is the following

Will this change make my organizational life better? Or, will this change make my organizational life worse?

Your employees want to know why the change that you want to make is in their best interests, individually.

In other words, every employee is listening to you talk

about your change effort and asking the following: What is in it for me?

To gain your employees real commitment to work with you to implement change — instead of against you — you must give them a believable answer to the above questions.

In addition, you also need to address the following:

- Why is the change better than what the organization is currently doing?
- How does the change benefit the work group?
- How does the change benefit the employees individually (in other words what is in it for them personally)?
- Why should this change happen now (as compared to dealing with this issue at a later point in time)?

When you address these critical information areas, you create your own sense of urgency by providing a believable and sensible explanation that answers the following:

1. Why the current way of doing things is no longer acceptable
2. Why the change that you want to make is better (for everyone concerned) than the current way of doing things

To answer these questions and to address the reasons why your employees are resisting your change effort, you will need to do some pre-work with your boss, peers, and employees as necessary.

Let's revisit the Change Scenario that we discussed in Chapter 1.

Change Scenario: What Should Have Been Done

Had John did a root-cause analysis before introducing his plan to implement new software, he would have been able to do some important pre-work before the meeting. This pre-work would have allowed him to answer their questions effectively.

His pre-work efforts would have identified the following:

- Having identified that his resident expert employee might be resistant to losing his status, John would have already identified a viable future role for his talented employee. With a viable alternative role, John could have countered his resistance from his resident expert.
- Having identified that most of his employees were cynical about future change efforts, John would have done prior work to develop a more efficient implementation process for his change effort. With a better process to implement change, John could have countered the resistance from his cynical employees.
- Having identified that his information technology employees were receptive to using new software, John would have given them a key role in the initial review with the vendor. With their inclusion in reviewing the software and with the introduction of a better change implementation process, John could have countered their resistance to support his change effort openly.

The above Case Scenario analysis shows that the key to effective change communication requires identifying the root cause of employee resistance to change.

Once you have done the root cause analysis, you can then present a well-crafted change communication message to your employees. Your well-crafted message will both anticipate the areas of employee resistance and provide alternative perspectives for them to consider.

With credible alternative perspectives, you can move your employees from resisting you to supporting you.

Key Points

Communicating the benefits of a change effort with a message that is both convincing and sensible is a powerful tool for stopping employee resistance to change.

Here are some key points for developing an effective change communication message:

- Communicating with your group that senior leadership is requiring change is most useful for gaining their initial attention that change is necessary. Avoid overusing this message however as this can backfire.
- Whenever you direct an employee to make changes he or she wants to know (1) will this change make my organizational life better or (2) will this change make my organizational life worse.
- To gain the continuing cooperation of your employees for your change effort you will have to address how the change is beneficial to the group AND how it is beneficial to them individually.

Benefit Analysis: Explaining the Value of Your Change Effort©

Overview

Effective communication is an important tool for stopping employee resistance to change. Communication is important because your team cannot effectively support a change effort that they do not understand. Your communication will answer why your change is necessary, how the change will benefit everyone, and why the change has to occur now.

Instructions

In this activity, you will gather critical information to use to communicate the importance of your change effort to your employees. As you complete the worksheet on the following page, think objectively about your change effort. Be careful to avoid overselling it in the answers you provide to the questions.

Also, keep in mind what you know that you can achieve in your organization given your leadership role, your influence with your peers and senior leadership, and your allocated resources.

Once you complete the worksheet, use this information in your communication with your employees about the benefits of your change effort.

Worksheet: Explaining the Value of Your Change Effort©

---

1. What is the reason for this change? (Explain the reasons why the current situation is no longer acceptable.)

2. What is the benefit of this change for the employees as a group AND for the employees individually? (How will the change improve workplace operations? Be specific and add business, industry, and customer data that proves your position as applicable.)

3. Why should this change happen now? (What is the reason why delaying this change is harmful to the company, group, etc.?)

The object of rewards is to encourage; if rewards are high then what the ruler wants will be quickly effected. (Han Fei)

3 RESISTANCE TO CHANGE: HOW MANAGERS CAN SUCCEED

Neutralizing Resistance to Change

An insightful approach to neutralize resistance to change is to find ways to make your change effort rewarding. If implemented correctly, rewards can be an important tool for keeping your employees supportive of your change effort.

Integrating rewards with your change effort works because rewards are something of value to your employees that you can give them in return for their contributions to your change effort (Reward, n.d.).

For rewards to be an effective response to employee resistance to change, however, they have to come from two sources. Rewards must come both from the organization and from completion of the actual work.

Extrinsic rewards come from the organization. They exist outside of the work that your employees complete.

Examples of extrinsic rewards include the following:
- Bonuses
- Promotions
- Ability to work from home
- Ability to work from anywhere
- Time flexibility
- Professional development opportunities
- Perks (10 Top Perks and Benefits That Win Employees Over, 2016)

For example, one extrinsic reward you could give your employees for meeting a critical change outcome is incentive bonus pay.

Other examples of extrinsic rewards you can consider include the following:
- Giving your employees an afternoon or day off from work
- Taking your employees to lunch or dinner
- Sponsoring a team building activity such as a catered picnic in a park or a departmental sports activity
- Having your boss or another senior level executive open your team meeting by thanking your team personally for their efforts (Excerpts from "1001 Ways to Reward Employees" By Bob Nelson, 2011)
- Providing a choice of a gift certificate from their favorite retailer (the amount does not have to be large)

These are just a few examples of extrinsic rewards that could work with a change reward program.

Intrinsic rewards are also critical to an effective change reward program. However, these rewards come from the work itself. In other words, your employees receive these rewards when they do their work.

Examples of intrinsic rewards include the following:
- Challenging work
- Participation in operational decision making

- Positive feedback for completion of the work
- Autonomy to choose methods for completion of the work
- Organizational respect for excellent performance
- Opportunity to collaborate with others on interesting work
- Opportunity to learn and do more (Tanner, Robert, 2018)

For example, one intrinsic reward you could give your employees for meeting a critical change outcome is a written letter of appreciation describing their specific contributions.

Other specific examples of intrinsic rewards you can consider include the following:

- Conducting weekly change implementation meetings with your employees where you collaborate with them on how best to meet the change outcomes
- Assigning specific change implementation duties to your employees (such as progress monitoring, industry research, customer consultation, preparing reports, reporting results)
- Allowing your employees to collaborate together and present recommendations to you on how to solve a problem that arises with the change effort
- Creating a visible progress board for others in your organization to see that highlights team and individual contributions to the change effort
- Expanding the role of your team members with new duties once the change effort is implemented

These are just a few examples of intrinsic rewards that could work with a change reward program.

Keep in mind that an effective rewards program that aligns with your change effort will have a blend of extrinsic and intrinsic rewards that are valuable to your employees.

Transforming Employee Resistance into Employee Support

Highly effective leaders use an insider secret to transform employee resistance into employee support.

This insider secret is a useful tool that is simple to apply to your change effort. It focuses on developing and using rewards that cover three core psychological areas.

In groundbreaking research, the Harvard psychologist, David McClelland developed a motivation theory about the three core psychological needs that all humans possess (David McClelland, n.d.). This motivation theory provides a simple but effective roadmap on actions managers can take to promote employee motivation.

With a little fine-tuning, we can use McClelland's Three Needs Theory to transform employee resistance into employee support.

Here is the principle of the Three Needs Theory:
>Human beings have varying needs for achievement, affiliation, and power. Employees with a **high-achievement need** want to solve problems and challenge themselves with difficult tasks. They are goal oriented, task focused, and they desire recognition.
>
>Employees with a **high-affiliation need** want acceptance and productive working relationships with others. They desire social interaction and cooperation in the workplace.
>
>Finally, employees with a **high-power need** want to have control and influence over their environment. They desire to be influential in a group or to be responsible for others (Tanner, Robert, 2018).

An important qualification about the Three Needs Theory is the fact that different employees will have varying needs for each of these areas.

Here is what successful leaders do to integrate the Three Needs Theory into their motivation efforts:

Since motivational factors differ from one employee to another, a manager must first identify the **three**-need profiles of those employees working with [him or] her before [he or] she can leverage these insights in the workplace. . . . [The manager can] focus on the different, high needs of [his or her] employees. This allows [the manager] to obtain [his or her] employees' cooperation. (Tanner, Robert, 2018)

To integrate the Three Needs Theory with your change rewards program, you will want to use a combination of intrinsic and extrinsic rewards that provide achievement, affiliation, and power opportunities for your employees.

Let's revisit the Change Scenario from Chapter 1, to see how managers can use rewards to address employee resistance to change.

Change Scenario: Getting it Right

After identifying the reasons why his employees were resistant to his efforts to implement the new software, John did some critical analysis of what he needed to do to neutralize their resistance to change.

John was an emotionally intelligent manager (Tanner, Robert, 2018). He realized that he launched his change effort with insufficient planning and with inadequate consultation with his employees. Due to his rushed implementation approach, John understood that he planted the seed, himself, for his employees' resistance.

John was not the type of manager to accept defeat, however. He decided to fix his change launch strategy. After his re-evaluation, he decided to address his employees' resistance strategically. To do this, he would make them an active part of a rewarding change implementation process.

Focusing on the different reasons why his employees were resistant to implementing the new software, John made the following individual interventions:

Resident Expert (reason for resistance: loss of status or job security in the organization)

As an *intrinsic, high-power* reward, John appointed this expert as the Subject Matter Expert (SME) for the change implementation. This effectively made his expert an assistant project lead working directly with John.

As an *extrinsic, high-achievement* reward, John identified a future potential promotion for the expert that would expand his current role to include oversight of training, quality assurance, and troubleshooting. This reward was conditional on the successful implementation of the software.

These rewards quieted the resident expert's resistance to the change effort. By keeping the expert close to him in the project implementation, John also prevented the expert from sabotaging the effort.

Finally, John identified a viable promotional opportunity for the expert (that also benefited the department). By doing this, John put a personal incentive in the change implementation for the expert to support implementation of the new software.

Information Technology (IT) Employees (reason for resistance: peer pressure)

As an *intrinsic, high-affiliation* reward, John assigned his IT employees the task of working directly with the software vendor and the employees to assess how to integrate the new software with the department's current processes.

After holding several meetings with the external vendor, the resident expert, and the remaining departmental employees, John's IT employees prepared a report of recommendations from the staff for implementing the software.

As an *extrinsic, high-affiliation* reward, John purchased pizza and soda for the meetings the IT employees held with their peers to complete the assessment.

These rewards subdued the IT employees' resistance to the change effort.

By giving the IT employees the autonomy to work with the vendor, the IT employees were able to understand the software functionality. With this information, the IT employees were then able to bond directly with the resident expert and the departmental employees (their peers) to identify how best to use the software.

By purchasing refreshments for the IT employees' meetings, John created a positive team environment that allowed his employees to form a cohesive group effort built around a successful implementation of the software.

Departmental Employees (reason for resistance: climate of mistrust)

As an *intrinsic, high-power* reward, John created bi-weekly team meetings for the change implementation with all of his employees. In these meetings, everyone openly discussed the software implementation, developed implementation timelines, and solved problems.

Prior to each meeting, John asked all of his employees to submit agenda items to him on issues that they wanted to discuss. He also had team members give regular updates on the status of their change implementation assignments.

As an *extrinsic, high-affiliation* reward, John celebrated the completion of major change implementation milestones with social events. He varied the rewards and they included taking the employees to lunch, having everyone bring in some food for a departmental potluck, and taking the afternoon off for a day in the park to play games and eat.

These rewards subdued the resistance of the departmental employees.

By creating bi-weekly team meetings and allowing the employees to submit agenda items, John made the employees co-owners with him of the change effort.

The employees now had direct impact on how the department implemented the change. With this power, this gave these employees an incentive to see the change implementation succeed.

Finally, by taking the employees to lunch to celebrate major change accomplishments, John kept the team cohesive and committed to implementing the new software.

John successfully transformed his employees from resisting him to supporting him. He also learned a critical leadership lesson. Leaders can share power with their employees and still maintain control.

You can prepare a change rewards program for your employees using the Worksheet at the end of this chapter. (The instructions are on the worksheet.)

Key Points

As the Kotter Leading Change Model explains, a critical step to leading change is to provide a picture of a future (after the change effort) that looks appealing and sensible (Tanner, Robert, 2018).

As the leader of your employees, a powerful tool to make your change effort appealing and sensible is to identify and use change rewards. By using appropriate rewards that are both extrinsic and intrinsic, you have the power to change how employees see your change effort.

Here are some key points for building an effective change rewards program:

- Extrinsic rewards come from the organization. They exist outside of the work that your employees complete.
- Intrinsic rewards come from the work itself. In other words, your employees receive these rewards when they do their work.
- Extrinsic and intrinsic rewards in the psychological areas of achievement, affiliation, and power can transform employee resistance to employee support.

Change Implementation Analysis: Building a Powerful Change Rewards Program©

WORSHEET: Building a Powerful Change Rewards Program©			
Use this worksheet to develop a rewards program for your change effort. Use one row for each of your employees. Note: As you identify rewards, focus on (1) what you can do within your scope of authority OR on (2) what you believe you can get your boss and others (if necessary) to support.			
Employee Description	**Three Needs Preference** (achievement/affiliation/power)	**Intrinsic Reward(s)** (comes from the work itself)	**Extrinsic Rewards** (comes from the organization)
Identify the employee by name. List the primary reason(s) why this employee is resistant to your change effort.	Identify the employee's top preference. *(Which of the three needs is most important to him or her?)*	Focusing on the employee's three need preference, identify several intrinsic rewards that you can provide to this employee.	Focusing on the employee's three need preference, identify several extrinsic rewards that you can provide to this employee.

©Copyright. Business Consulting Solutions LLC. All Rights Reserved Worldwide.

Never doubt that a small group of committed people can change the world. Indeed it is the only thing that ever has. (Margaret Mead)

CONCLUSION

In 2010, the technology research and advisory firm, Gartner, published a report on the changing nature of work. Specifically, they predicted then that managers will "need to plan for increasingly chaotic environments that are out of their direct control and adaptation" (Egham, 2010).

Gartner's predictions turned out to be farsighted!

As they noted, organizational work is less routine, employees work more frequently in permanent and temporary team structures, and external groups have more impact on the success or failures of businesses (Tanner, Robert, 2018).

As Gartner predicted, it is certain that you are managing in chaotic times. The harsh truth is that chaos and disruption in the workplace are now a normal fact of organizational life.

This change in the workplace means that your ability to get your employees to work with you — instead of against you — will directly affect your own career success. It also means that you do not have the option of being ineffective at stopping employee resistance to change. Overcoming employee resistance to change is a required leadership skill; it is no longer a nice-to-have skill.

For this reason, it is critical that you approach change proactively.

Approaching change proactively requires you to do the following:

1. Anticipate the reasons why your employees may resist you
2. Validate your reasoning for their resistance with evidence
3. Develop a targeted communication and change rewards strategy

As you do the hard work to address employee resistance to change, keep in mind that people do not naturally resist change.

The more that you can credibly show your employees that change is good for the group AND good for them individually, the easier it will be for you to stop resistance to change.

ACCESS TO END OF CHAPTER TOOLS

NOTE: To receive a PDF version of the end-of chapter application tools in this book, go to this website address: https://goo.gl/MhGFVZ.
This link is for your use only. Please do not share it with anyone else. Thank you

ADDITIONAL RESOURCES

The information on the following pages contains additional leadership resources.

Cheat Sheet: 4 Insider Secrets to Counteract Resistance to Change©

1	Identify the reasons why employees are resisting your change effort. This will allow you to develop a proactive strategy to respond appropriately to them.
2	Develop a sensible and persuasive communication message of a clear reason for your change effort. This is critical to gaining team member cooperation.
3	Avoid using force continually to get your employees to obey your directives to change. This will prevent you from harming morale and causing further employee resistance to change.
4	Ensure that your change has benefits for your employees as a group and for them individually. This will help you to gain their cooperation for your change effort.

Cheat Sheet: 5 Best Practices for Effectively Communicating Your Change Effort©

	Keep it Simple Use simple and specific language to communicate your change message. Avoid jargon and generalities.
	Repeat the Message Find appropriate situations in your daily operations to repeat your change message.
	Use Multiple Methods Use various communication methods (verbal, written, digital) to explain your change message.
	Make it Two-Way As you communicate, ask questions, listen to understand, and clarify what you heard. Spend more time listening to others than speaking yourself.
	Make it Positive Without over promising, explain your change goals in terms of the benefits they will bring.

Chart: Why People Resist Change©

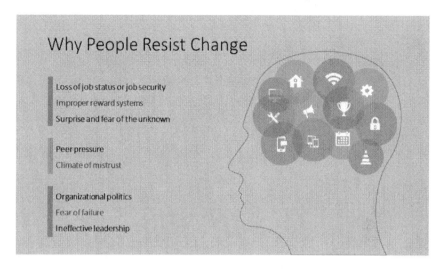

LINKS TO LEADERSHIP RESOURCES

Leadership Videos: My Management is a Journey YouTube Channel provides quick, visually appealing, and easy-to-understand videos on leadership and management topics. You can visit my YouTube Channel at the URL: www.youtube.com/user/MgmtJourney.

Leadership Blog: My Management is a Journey Blog provides practical leadership and management articles to help you with the people side of the business. You can visit my blog at the URL: https://ManagementisaJourney.com

---

Leadership Books: I have more leadership books available on Amazon. To learn more about these books, you can visit my Amazon Author page at the URL: www.amazon.com/Robert-Tanner/e/B00KC7CAJU/ref=dp_byline_cont_ebooks_1.

ABOUT THE AUTHOR

Robert Tanner is the Founder and Principal Consultant of Business Consulting Solutions LLC, based in the state of Washington. He is also the author of the popular leadership blog, Management is a Journey®.

Robert is a leadership professional with 20+ years of real-world experience at all levels of management. He helps managers with the people side of the business focusing on leadership and management development, interpersonal effectiveness, and change leadership.

Robert has a MBA degree in Strategic Management and a BS degree in Organizational Behavior. He is a certified change management consultant, a top rated national trainer, and a certified practitioner of behavioral type assessments (Myers-Briggs, DISC Profiles, etc.). He is also a former Adjunct Professor of Management at the graduate and undergraduate levels and a lifetime member of the international honor society, Beta Gamma Sigma.

Business Site: BusinessConsultingSolutionsLLC.com

Leadership Blog: ManagementisaJourney.com

DISCLAIMER

All the material contained in this book is provided for educational and informational purposes only. Links were functional when this book was published. Images are used with permission.

While every attempt has been made to provide information that is both accurate and effective, the author and Business Consulting Solutions LLC do not assume any responsibility for the use or misuse of this information. All leadership activity requires careful evaluation of the organizational context and of the personalities and experiences of the affected organizational stakeholders. As you review the information in this book, only you can determine what will be useful to you and your organization.

The author and Business Consulting Solutions LLC are not rendering a professional service and therefore can take no responsibility for any results or outcomes resulting from the use of this material.

USE OF THIS MATERIAL

This is commercial copyrighted material. You cannot use it for your own commercial purposes, post it on your website for distribution to others, share it on social media, and otherwise use or present this work as your own material.

REFERENCES

10 Top Perks and Benefits That Win Employees Over. (2016, April 13). Retrieved from Robert Half: https://www.roberthalf.com/blog/compensation-and-benefits/10-top-perks-and-benefits-that-win-employees-over

Berkman, Olivia. (2018, March 28). There's A Difference Between Disruption and Chaos and You Need Strategies for Both. Retrieved from Financial Executives International: https://daily.financialexecutives.org/theres-difference-disruption-chaos-need-strategies/

David McClelland. (n.d.). Retrieved from Harvard University Department of Psychology: https://psychology.fas.harvard.edu/people/david-mcclelland

Egham, U. (2010, August 4). Gartner Says the World of Work Will Witness 10 Changes During the Next 10 Years. Retrieved from Gartner: https://www.gartner.com/newsroom/id/1416513

Excerpts from "1001 Ways to Reward Employees" By Bob Nelson. (2011, August). Retrieved from University of Washington Facilities Services: https://facilities.uw.edu/orgrel/files/documents/recognition/recognition_1001.pdf

Reward. (n.d.). Retrieved from Dictionary.com: http://www.dictionary.com/browse/reward

Tanner, Robert. (2017, March 13). Five Ways Employees Both Get Mad and Get Even. Retrieved from Management is a Journey: https://managementisajourney.com/five-ways-employees-both-get-mad-and-get-even/

Tanner, Robert. (2017, March 2). The Ugly Truth About Why People Naturally Resist Change. (Hint: They Don't!). Retrieved from Management is a Journey:

https://managementisajourney.com/the-ugly-truth-about-why-people-naturally-resist-change-hint-they-dont/

Tanner, Robert. (2018, April 7). How the World of Work is Changing (Part 1). Retrieved from Management is a Journey: https://managementisajourney.com/how-the-world-of-work-is-changing-part-1/

Tanner, Robert. (2018, February 7). Intrinsic Rewards – You'll Need More Than Money and Benefits! Retrieved from Management is a Journey: https://managementisajourney.com/intrinsic-rewards-youll-need-more-than-money-and-benefits/

Tanner, Robert. (2018, February 7). Kotter's Eight Step Leading Change Model. Retrieved from Management is a Journey: https://managementisajourney.com/summary-of-kotters-eight-step-leading-change-model/

Tanner, Robert. (2018, March 30). Leading Change (Step 1): Creating a Sense of Urgency. Retrieved from Management is a Journey: https://managementisajourney.com/leading-change-step-1-creating-a-sense-of-urgency/

Tanner, Robert. (2018, February 5). Motivation – As Simple As The Three Needs Theory. Retrieved from Management is a Journey: https://managementisajourney.com/motivation-as-simple-as-the-three-needs-theory/

Tanner, Robert. (2018, March 1). Organizational Change: 8 Reasons Why People Resist Change. Retrieved from Management is a Journey: https://managementisajourney.com/organizational-change-8-reasons-why-people-resist-change/

Tanner, Robert. (2018, March 15). What is Emotional Intelligence and Why is it Important? Retrieved from Management is a Journey: https://managementisajourney.com/what-is-emotional-intelligence-and-why-is-it-important/

Whack-a-Mole. (2018, March 28). Retrieved from Wiktionary: https://en.wiktionary.org/wiki/whack-a-mole

Made in the USA
Columbia, SC
01 September 2019